Unspeakable Things.
A Small Collection of Confessional Poetry.

Written by Ave Maria Siobhan
Edited by Emily Price

Contents

For a calm that may follow.

Blue Spring, Headlights, Killing E.

Burn,
bright blue.
I burn into you.

I read like a poem.
I carry your corpse to my bedroom.
Watching through the window,
torture takes its time.

Daylight becomes new.
We are older—
in this,
together.
Separate from whatever came our way before.

In the terror, I can remember—

I'm watching you step across red tiling.
Separating us,
I take in your movements.
You stalk what I represent.

Unspoken things

shift between us.
Hands touch my shoulder blades.

The desirable sides of you
loom
in the doorway.

You're swaying on your feet,
hand on the railing.
The cigarette on your tongue goes out.

It's blue,
eyes wandering on a night in April.
I'm burning into you.
My ashes taste the back of your neck.

Your nothingness molds into the walls at night.

I dream of uncertain things,
of your arms around me.
I'm singing in the daytime.

Light touches,
eyes stay open.
I'm alone without you,
accompanying eternity.

Nothing I haven't thought of before,
nothing unseen.

If I find you,
again,
I will murder the parts of you that break me.

Don't hurt;
watch as I leave.
Headlights shine while you're still here.

Lilacs.

I.

I'm young,
It hurts me.
And

you are beautiful.
You are

so,
so beautiful.

He's got his gun out again.
Waving his fists in the air,
I hear him.

His words move through me;
nothing else stays
inside of my chamber.
Face on fire.
I never cry
in this circumstance.

He steps up into his silver truck.
When he speaks,
I hear half of what scares me.

The drive home satiates
what thirst stays behind my teeth.

Black gun.
Dark jeans.
Jesus in the walls.

II.

In his vicinity,
two windows rest.
Flies begin to decay
under the sun,
in the cracks of the sill.

Winter does not breathe.
Spring makes love
to a devotional summer.

During her wake,
blossoms form on the tree outside.
I see it on a sunny day,

it becomes everything to me.

He takes me home,
eventually.

III.

I'm still
when Jesus rests there.

Inside is hellfire.
Unwilling,
I'm weak if I'm not deaf.

Like angels
falling to earth.

IV.

In the front yard of his house,
there's a lilac tree.

The only assurance
that spring would bring sweet nothingness.

I stand outside during May,

smelling the air.

I'm young,
it hurts me.
And

you are beautiful.
You are

so,
so beautiful.

We remain in silence—
hearing nothing of what scares me.
I find him in the changing circle,
to be alone after his worsening.

He puts his gun away.

His despair holds me
as time continues.

He makes us leave.
A visit to see lilac travesties,
so sweet in recollection.

In Bloom.

Her mother cries when provoked.

Gentle. Fingers touch her freckled cheek. I'm kissing her temple. Our hair tangles. She coddles me.

I crawled from womb to ground. She loved me as one could love a corpse— obsessive, self-righteous praise. Needs diminished, she never held me for more than a moment. Never told me how beautiful things were going to be.

What else could there have been to say? If you were there, I could've known you better.

If only, I could've known better.

The Wall.

It's almost nine.
Embers,
the fabric inside
the folding chair drink holder.

Calm air.
Fingers stuck
between teeth and wood.

I've got eyes
on his guitar strings.
He sings something taught to me,
then.

I speak what I can.

Warm breeze holds me in my tenderness.
Time does not require me,
I am new to everything.

It is quiet,
shy.

I don't know where he comes from.

He's young.
He's got hair
like David Cassidy.
He's gone by breakfast.

He has a wife,
my less familiar family.
I see her walking down a private road.
I hear stories—
photographed in time.

He's smiling with the sun behind his teeth.
He's got no other place to be than here.

He gets older,
the embers die out.

I see him at a family wedding.
He's tall,
gentle demeanor.
I'm standing by a barn overlooking a mountain.

We talk
because I'm terrified.

In time,

his wife passes.
I don't see him.
I hear stories of him
driving off
on his motorcycle.
The sun gets trapped
somewhere under his helmet.

I get news in the summer.
Thirteen years had passed,
after all.

I'm staring down at this polaroid of him.
I see him in the 70s.

He finds the sun in his lungs.
He dies when I'm eighteen.

I lose myself with him.
I lose small hands,
waves by the rocks.

I am silent,
older.
Time bleeds with me.
Summer turns to fall.

I visit graveyards filled with strangers.
I recover within a day.

I'm sorry,
eternally,
that nothing can stay.

Reverent (to the Archangel).

You make me blush.

Layers of skin,
hardened with ancient philosophies,
peel back

to reveal something less ruthless.

Your fingertips are dipped
in a true scarlet.
Your hands are bathed in sanctuary
and dancing lamentation.

A reckless trilogy of moonlit sacrifice,
resurrection,
budding nihilism.

Unholy Archangel,
you stood willingly.

Sculpted bodies
waited to take flight
as some night owl shrieked.

Ravenous songbird.

Lovely to take you
in whatever form.

I yearned for the ink draping
the small of your back.
The voyeur's feast,
midnight delusions—
how irresponsible.
A holy war waged in sweat
and exhaled as grit,
when the earth cradled you
as a broken infant.

And all you saw were a pair of eyes,
golden, darting back and forth.

Golden and weeping
lavender tears.

Somewhere it became all but
a fragment.
My own fantasy
of some midsummer
wrongdoing.

Some unspeakable act remained quiet,
in the air,
as I choked on the daybreak.

You took me by the unwashed hands.
Immaculate,
I kissed your flesh.

The angel faded
into some inglorious
reflection.
And you were one
with the dirt
you hailed from.

I counted to seven,
hushed,
trembling from the misery
of the songbird's cry.

There was the recollection,
how surely—
how absolute.

How a pair of wandering eyes

paved some uncertain way
to the depraved promise land.

How the desolate
Christ figure
soothed you.

With undoubted subtlety,
she spoke:

*Never rot away,
delicate muse,
longing and deserted.*

*Lest we all die
of the scripture
left unwritten.*

La Madonna.

She's fixing her hair in the rearview mirror.
I'm seeing her in action—
it's magic,
a cheap, pit-stop kind.
She open carries,
cracks jokes,
smokes by the creek.

On a different evening,
I'm tucked into her blue cardigan.
It's unwashed.
Her hair smells like lemongrass.

She's obscene—
I love her in a way that won't last.

I'm waking up on rough sheets,
wool picked up from Lancaster.
She's drinking Earl Grey with lavender.

From the driver's seat,
she watches the sunrise on the lake.
She doesn't pay attention to me.
I press my ear against the floor of the van.

We're so close.
I hear her heartbeat in the floorboards.
I feel the divinity buried in her spine.

She's spectacular under moonlight.

I see her spitting
with dirt smeared across her face.
She's under the bridge
humming a tune I don't know.

Things are good for a week or two.
I touch the back of her shoulder
as we race through the forest.
In Wilson,
we watch the sunset on a boulder.
Neither of us speak.

She ends up with this song in her throat,
too low for me to hear.

It's June one day.
I'm sitting on a porch,
passing a joint to her best friend.

She tells me I'll always have a home there.

It's the last time I see her.

It's better the love never reached her.

E.B.A.

I write you into my dreams,
as if you were meant for something more
gorgeous in my life.

You store your vices
under the corners of a mattress.
I undress by the windows,
waiting for your signal.

You're concerned.
I don't promise you the morning,
nothing wakes me like that.

Don't look at the mess
you leave,
strewn across curtains,
dusty floorboards.

You are broken into brilliant pieces,
shattering against stained drywall.

In your sleeplessness,
I place you back together.

I'm unable to see your intimacy.
I don't wait to leave.

You promise so much,
to not let anything go.

There's a vision I welcome,
toward the end.

I'm standing on a grassy hill.
I've got my arm around your waist—
things are stoic.

I am your man.
I'm your woman.

Through your skin,
I feel wolves' teeth against my palms.
You are dangerous
to me.

You are the unwanted thing
sleeping at the edge of my memory.

On a day long ago.

You speak.
I don't know what listening is.

Corner me into lucidity.
Break me open.
Read me like a wound,
please.

Ash & Bone.

Confessional in everything.
I scrub myself of him after every evening.

Second nature,
after a while.

I'm dirty,
he's in worse condition.
I am lyrical and unstable.
He's brutal by the minute.

I cannot do this with him.

He speaks a language
I've been hungering for.

Taking his anger,
I nurture the flame.
Waiting for something to catch—

I smell like fucking menthols,
too much like spiced rum and sweat.
Our hollowed faces greet each other.
He's asking for a smoke.

By the railing,
sighing,
desperation floods his eyes.

I will not do this for him.

I take him in my vulnerability,
hoping to leave him
somewhere undefined.
My sternum feels the heaviness of him there.

This time, I don't hide from the enemy.
I'm on my knees,
scrubbing pieces of him from the earth.

He asks me to be there for him
so he can survive—
so he doesn't have to find someone else.
So he won't turn back to heroin.
In his words,
these are all sacrifices.

Confessional in what he desires to be true.
I don't know him,

never once did I know him.

With passion,
I willingly die from something I could let go of.

I won't have him do this to me.

I could've imagined how this would end.

I feel unwelcome here.
Drunk again,
walking around what he destroyed.

He promises nothing.
I'll promise myself better,
next time.

I can no longer love his deceit.

This is the original language,
one that does not starve its listeners.
From this,
I must break away by force.

In the throes of early mornings,
he's there, taking from me.
I once loved what he could be.

Though,
I am enough for this.
I have had enough of this,

Dearest.

Dies Irae.

Unspoken.
I will take you.
In whatever form you arrive,
I will embrace you.

Unthought of.
You murdered your reflection
this morning.
The lost arrival to a man—

in everything,

only a man.

How cruel it was.
I wept for you,
twirled as you struck a minor chord.

Danced around your silhouette
while the earth inhaled.

Hiding all they had once said to you:

Never rot away

lest we all die.

Lest there were a more
hideous form of suffering
than to watch you stir
in your unmarked grave.

I looked on
as the last of your innocence
ran from golden eyelids.

How often
I wept for you
only to attract your unnatural stare.

There could not have been
a more painful torture
than to watch you molt from your vessel
and fly toward the sun—

Icarus adored you the same.

My reverence is deserted,
I cannot have you.
My songbird has been cannibalized,
I cannot trust you.

From the unruly dawn,
I breathed into you.

I have died.

I questioned if you knew any better.
If your finger stroked the wrong key—
only to have you collapse as I tore away.

You will not be resurrected anymore.
Your throat will shut.
I will listen to you play
your last sonata
with deaf ears.

Blind eyes
falling upon a once-divine masterpiece.

Unsafe.
David stares back into me,
but I can only sense the wasted sorrow.

And by God,
when there's nothing
left

to remember you by—

I will scream when you are gone.

I will hold myself under the weight
of your ivory heartbreak,
let them bury me
in a wooden casket.

If only to be last,
captured in a silent cry.

Clutching at my throat
next to your corpse.

And as the trumpets sound,
Gabriel will advance on me.

I'll shift myself awake
one million times,
feeling nothing more
than what could've been.

A hallowed cry from heaven.

You're all that's left in the ashes.

And when she spoke—
some unruly dusk,
under lavender lighting—

Your lips separated.
Your hands trembled against
a merciless
magnum opus.

With undoubted subtlety,
She'd said to you:

Delicate muse,
longing and deserted.

You have digressed,
and I will never harm you again.

The holy war has been waged;
lost in the debris,
I am here.

I am here to sing,
to feel your absence.

And it is the completed scripture.
This is the end.

And you will never love me
as much as I could've loved you.

Unholy Archangel,
ravenous songbird.

Lovely to take you
in whatever form.

This is the end,
and I wanted to tear you apart.

This is the end,
and I wanted to take you.

Perfected with empty promises,
I wanted you with me.

You faded
into some inglorious
reflection.

And you were one

with the dirt
you hailed from.

Though it will never be enough,
if you gave the earth a second to breathe,
you'd hear me calling for you.

This is the end.
This is all I have left.

My inescapable,
undeniable

wrath of God.

Vacant (Orchids).

I.

As she walked
naked
through the moonlit path,

she spoke in the first language.

Conditioned to evaluate each lover
as if they were a severed memory.

Her ancient metaphors won't salvage the wreck,
yet such deceit
will be cleansed—

pure—

as soon as the sun rises.

But it hurts when she hates me.
It hurts when she hunts me down,
sweat sticking to the corners of my face.

I'm a painting once lived for and inspired—

now lost to the ruined masses of starving eyes.

I lie awake,
vacant,
my back against hers.
I close my eyes and see a new version of you.

II.

It's raw in the city,
painful and dry,
yet always eternal.

Clouds embrace the moonlight—
I reminisce on a night we were both exposed.

I see a painting where she is new;
she is spent.
She has unkempt hair and loves broken women.

Oh,
I can't be that broken woman
left spiraling.
A lust
for a love,
devoid of grace.

You're never up when you're up.
You're never wrong when you're wrong.
It's always the fault of the other party,
darling.

I knew that.

III.

The sun set while I slept in the back of a car.
I dreamt of the devil holding me.
About hemorrhaging in his embrace.
My eyes ran crimson against his skin.

I dreamt about absent ceremonies,
the wake of a death never experienced.

I let you fuck me that night.
Bruised legs under cold sheets.
I wanted your nails dug into my collarbones.
I wanted your blood staining my thighs
as I drank from your river.

IV.

You tell me you hate it here with me, in Virginia.
I don't blame you.

I close my eyes and you're a painting.
You're staring through me,
watching her golden silhouette
take me by the heart.

I am *ruptured,*
disturbed,

wrong.

I am kissing you with my car window rolled down.
I am absent-minded.
You slip between my fingers so quickly.
It's an unfair game.

If I could have it any other way,
I'd have us walking that beach,
laughing and heaving.
Taking in the ocean air.

If I could have it any other way,
I'd be asleep in my own bed.

If I could have it any other way,
I'd urge you
to light my skin on fire.
To breathe the smoke from my lips.

The country is old,
tired.
I know that.

But I'll still find my ways to you.
I'll still sing about the rolling hills that led us back home.
I'll still feel your skin against my teeth,
against my tongue.

It's still evident:
you terrify me.

Enough.

To prove to myself
I am alive.

Bury your mistrust with me.
Tell me the smaller secrets in your life.

V.

I am lost,
here.
It's my stop,
my time to leave.

Every woman that passed you by
only dedicated themselves to men.

I preach the same,
trailing past fragile masculinity
with starving eyes.

If I were him,
things wouldn't be this way.
There'd be no women
wishing I were kinder,
more understanding.
There'd be no women to love me.

There'd just be women.
There'd just be hands to touch me.
To hold me,
like you held him.

If I woke up and you were gone,

I wouldn't blame you.

You hate it here.
I don't blame you.

VI.

You're different again.
Towering,
with hair that embraces your hips.

You're blind to me.
I'm sorry.

You're different again.
Pale.
With thin wrists
and violet claws.

It's desolate where you are.
I'm sorry.

The woman I'd loved for a year,
I don't know your name anymore.

I'll try to be better.

I'll try to be easier with my hands as the months go on.

But it hurts when she hates me.

It hurts,
after everything.

You are new,
now.

You are old,
now.

Hiems.

I find myself on the other side.
Eyelids shut,
you listen to rain—
I scrub stained hands
under dim lighting.

Gentle,
healing
all you embrace.

You wake up to cherish pain,
you're met with a tenderness
which hurts you most.

And though you are gentle,
the stages of your seasons
only do you harm.

Solutions to your problems
rely on the destruction
of your nectar and vow.
I will try to care
as to not let it go to waste.

I know you're beautiful in real life.

I'll kill myself to avoid your winter.
I'll cry another merciful aria,
I refuse to sacrifice you again.
I refuse to lose you
in my own blind darkness.
One more time.

One more time.

Your heart will beat another day.
I'll be against you in a bathtub
with wrinkled palms and quiet apathy.
I'll ask to stroke the contours of your face,
to press my chin into the crook of your neck.
I'll ask to trace the curve of your waist
as we lay parallel in darkness.

Against you,
I will whisper:

There is nothing more arousing than confusion.
Than vulnerability to a potential lover.

I will stand for the most sorrowful show,

applauding another hollow performance.

I can't trust a man for another exhausted cause.
They let me down with distant sighs.

I won't continue to weep.
I know the way a man works:
shifting, molding
into scars and a lasting appetite.

I'll let him fade away.
Fade out.
Let another promise
crawl his way into my lungs.

Yes,
I know.
Now
I know.

I trust your lips against my wrist.
Passing an abstract view as I dream,
certain.
While all is silent,
you are here,
holding me

under cold sheets.

I'll see you when I sleep again.
I'll mimic the positions of your naked flesh—
unsteady under moonlight,
long ago.
I'll wait for you to glide
upward into black oxygen.

I'm so sorry
to leave you like this.
I'm rightfully terrified,
this time around.

In due time,
I'll grow accustomed to the way your lips tremble.
You'll bite at pale skin,
ribs expanding under your teeth.

You are the most dangerous part of the process.
When everything changes.

I'll hold you under a tombstone in daylight,
melt into the cracks of your lips.
Strolling through cemeteries with bare hands,
you will belong to nature.

Eventually.

Every part of you will shatter into something new.
You will sink into bluebirds and late spring,
bathed in soil.
Embraced by the tears of virtues
and divine promise.

It'll nurse me.
I'm taught like this—
naturally,
hesitantly.

I was raised to believe men are men,
and women are men disguised by a soft gaze—
with the urge to take flight
at the nearest opportunity.

You cascade against an azure surface.
You are volatile and desperate for wings,
like others before you.
Spiraling.
Familiar to
this hollow existence.

None of it matters

when the last of it passes us,
you breathe into me.
Listening,
I stay so distant.

None of it could ever matter.

I'd sway with you in my arms,
burning adoration
into you.
Toss myself into familiar nihilism
when the sky becomes raw.
Recede into nothingness.

Left deserted,
Cold.
Separated,
Alone.
Away from all you ever were.

It's so cold.
It's so cold without you.

I turn violet,
handprints engraved
into heart and lungs.

Longing for the moment
you're carefully surrendered.

I face you,
a pale reflection
in the shadows of your heart.
Turn you a new shade of delicate,
placing lips to mumbled confessions.

I will be there when snow falls,
listening for a silent applause.

You're alone.
Waiting for the day
when I can give you something more.

I could promise to be your isolated matriarch.
I could promise you the brutality that accompanies
cloudless nights
and softer music.

I'd be there
with you.
Hidden under golden frames
and rusted bird cages.

I want it that way.
Serene.
Watering tomatoes with you
on a Monday morning.

You are a clear sky to me,
A soft pillow to place my head.

I will stare into you while the earth thaws,
until I am blinded by your sun.

With everything,
I promise.

When you are the most beautiful thing in my eyes,

I will drown under ice.
Seek an unknown
darkened torture,
to see another morning
where you are more than blue.
To recognize your eyes again
in different lighting,
this time around.

It's never fair where the winter takes you.

Gazing at broken mirrors,
I see you once more.

In the end,
you'll be all I need.

Blue.

I don't let it stay.
Almost small,
if I think about it enough.

I don't hear any part of what's being said.
Taste begins to have no meaning.
I am familiarized,
left to shadows,
when love dissipates.

I worry often.
If this is me.
Some cruel thing
I can breastfeed
for the sake of aching.
It burns a little more
as I awake.

This is a suicide note.
This is a release.

I am gray,
now.
You're off in fields

of benevolent dreams.

I sought after a person in a hospital.
Missed the hospital on nights
I didn't breathe.
Nights where terror was louder
than thought,
where ground turned to fire.

Pain is no longer easy to waste.
I grow to adore a sense of the lesser.

An organic malnourishment.

Happiness
falling down a mountainside.
Spilling onto
pine trees.

I ask you more than ten times.
It reaches twenty.
I still search for the answer.

The hell I brought you to in September.
Christmas Day.
January first.

Almost small,
if I don't think about it for long.

This is my confession to you.

I die
once more.
Horrendously,
magnificently.

You have me sing on the days
I bleed out.
You love me all the way to three in the morning.

I still think about you.
How I never saw you clearly.

At the edge,
I see every part of us,
sleeping under starry skies.

It shakes me,
still.

Ominea.

Grass is lush in her atmosphere.
In a hushed voice,
she sings to me.

Gray clouds keep me inside
with my blameless understanding.
Her vibrato sounds with the breeze.
She lets me live
in this period of wanting.

Sparrows swing and speak in the afternoon—
a freedom
I live to feel.

I live to dream about her in another color,
in blooming visions
of California poppies.
Longing for a moment of rest
in fields of yellow daisies.

I love her in my time.
Silent in my atmosphere;
she lives, vicariously, through my fragility.

Lupins begin to bloom in the backyard.
Sweat collects under my brow,
I run across the driveway after the dog.

By the field,
feet sink into the swimming hole.
Snakes thread themselves through the dandelions.
Finches gather at the pole.

Evening brings the smell of smoke.
I study movement outside
through the small windows.
It's an urgent hunger.

To escape from here—

Bare feet settle into the soil below.
I drift through unknown tree lines,
branches dancing with the wind.
Moss, up to my legs
in the deepest part of the creek.

Twilight speaks her wisdom.
She follows me,
wherever I run to.

In my atmosphere,
She rests silently.

Ready for every beautiful thing,
ready for any moment of anguish.
I step with caution
on this mountain path.

Peaceful
for a short time.
The smell of dusk,
visions of clover valleys,
baby's breath.

It's dark outside,
I feel her with every falling leaf.
She continues through the nighttime,
unwilling to look past my innocence.

The ocean washes me of her,
dragging my arms through a cold awakening.
The sand warms with the sun's arrival.
Thorn bushes catch my skin
as I head through the beach trails.

The world remains calm.

In Freedom,
There's a sunflower garden
near a graveyard.
I go there,
to be with the dead,
where she doesn't find me.

The birds meet me as a body.

As my loneliness.

As rebirth.

So I can find peace.
Flying over a mountainside,
swimming across rivers,
burning dead leaves under stars.

In my atmosphere.

*It's beautiful,
once the sun rises.*

Beautiful Things.

It doesn't leave me.

You are distant now.

Progress,
to the end
of a moving exhaustion.

To hear you,
to hold old journals.
Stirring dust

in the attic.
Rest tired wings on empty bottles.

The showerhead drips lukewarm
on her turning body.
She doesn't know I'm in the room,

writing by the fireplace.

I place myself inside her journals,
my own cemented poetry.

Sorting through her pages,
she speaks in cycles:

The closure of new relationships.
Love cannot be this way.

If it does not exist in plain sight—

She sleeps through the morning.
The door leans open,
quiet footsteps down wet asphalt
at sunrise.

Consciously searching for a new place
to rely on,
She reminds me I'm here.
Hungering for this.

Picking morning glories from the garden,
I sing like Adrianne,
wandering through tall grass.

Self-isolating.
Dull colors swim across the walls.
Silent current,
the plants breathe in my direction.

In the tree line,
stars sink to the earth like rain.

Oh,
I don't know anything.

I feel everything.

The bed sheets are softer than imagined.
Olive vines reach from the linen
through my hands—
my body has never been this light.
Shades of beautiful hold me
in place of her.
Things don't hurt like this,
often.

Dawn embraces the hills,
blue jays call through the branches outside.
Dishes go undone,
consciousness remains heavy.
She doesn't leave;
I don't return after breakfast.

Perpetuating his humanity,
he severs the cords of my loneliness.

His separation
will be the thing to kill me.

He sits
barefoot in the grass.
I scatter journals in front of him.

We've hurt each other,
I'm so sorry.
Nothing beautiful falls between us.
Never meant for anything.

In the love that is—

He packs an old suitcase.
He throws his part of the acid away.
Clothes go unfolded.

In June,
she lies next to me.
I want so badly to be in love with her.
Her memory brings the scent of lavender.

In August,
hair sticks to my neck.
Frogs gather on rocks outside.

Nighttime rain echoes on the roof.
I am in love with him.

By Cape Elizabeth,
she tries taking pictures in the sun.
Nothing comes out right.
She writes in journals I hear nothing about.

Nothing becomes anything.
Not that it could've.
It doesn't give you a life worthwhile.

Don't recognize her as that person anymore.
Let it be what hurts the most.

All parts of this,
my love breaks me.

Desire to know you,
nonetheless.
To care,
no matter the reason for our separation.

No matter the distance of what was,
or if I'll find you again.

All of these beautiful things—

I don't know the answers to
any of them.

A special appreciation for the love that is.

Emily Price is an editor specializing in non-fiction & poetry. She serves as a manuscript reviewer for Berrett-Koehler & as a literary journal reader for the Baltimore Review. Emily is a compassionate and professional editor, who expresses her passions through helping independent, beginning writers publish their work with confidence. In 2019, Price was the recipient of the Country Roads Magazine Young Writers Award.

***

Ave Siobhan is a Maine-based Cosmetologist & Makeup Artist, as well as a college undergraduate studying History. Growing up in remote areas throughout the state, Siobhan has spent their life exploring the vast wilderness Maine has to offer.